Finding our SPIRITUAL STRENGTH

Quotes from Emanuel Swedenborg

Selected by Basil Lazer

Translated by Lee Woofenden

Edited by Julian Duckworth

Note that the quotes in this book are selected sections
and in some cases are abridged. Sometimes examples given
within a quote to illustrate a concept have been changed
to more present-day versions to help make the concept
more easily understood by today's readers.

Finding Our Spiritual Strength: quotes from Emanuel Swedenborg

Selected by Basil Lazer
Translated by Lee Woofenden
Edited by Julian Duckworth
Designed by Donna Heldon

Illustrated by Donna Heldon
Illustrations are on pages 12, 38, 61, 67, 88, 94, 97, 100 and 108

Thank you to everyone who has been part of the creation of this book

---

Finding Our Spiritual Strength: quotes from Emanuel Swedenborg
is published by Our Shared Spirituality Press
www.oursharedspirituality.org

First edition published 2026
Based on the book *Shuning Evils as Sins (The Importance of Self
Examination)* by Basil Lazer, published 1981

Paperback ISBN 978-0-9756523-0-5
Ebook ISBN 978-0-9756523-1-2
PDF ISBN 978-0-9756523-2-9

A catalogue record for this
book is available from the
National Library of Australia

Welcome

Think of a moment that touched your soul, when suddenly, life was more meaningful. This profound feeling is explored here, inspired by unique spiritual insights shared by Emanuel Swedenborg, who wrote in detail about the highest form of good, which is what many people call God, the Bible's deeper meaning, and our life's true purpose.

The quotes in this book open up ways to gain a deeper understanding of ourselves. They offer spiritual guidance for clearing out things that hold us back, giving us space to choose things that take us forward. We then see that our own spiritual salvation is in fact a deeply personal and gradual rebirth. Realising the power we have in every choice we make is at the heart of our spiritual strength.

These insights illuminate our spiritual journeys, and we're excited to share them with you. Each quote shines on its own, paired with a brief reflection and a simple practice. Whether you read from beginning to end or wander through the pages, pausing where something catches your eye, this book offers real resources to help us all build up our spiritual strength.

Would you say that you're pretty much in touch with things like your thoughts, your feelings, your ups and downs?

How do you handle them, especially when it's not easy?

How well do you feel you know yourself?

Look at the book title for a moment ... *Finding Our Spiritual Strength*. We know what physical strength is. But ... spiritual strength? Strength in your values, beliefs, and your own self-worth, confident that you have found your true place.

A spiritual writer called Emanuel Swedenborg, who lived 300 years ago, shared profound spiritual insights that open up the inner world of spirituality for us. One of his great contributions was revealing the deep connections between God, our spiritual beliefs, and the personal, inner life we experience every day.

What takes our spiritual strength away from us is very often us falling into unhelpful thoughts, opinions and feelings. We all do it at times, and it can make us feel pretty bad about ourselves, or weak, certainly not strong. But even just knowing we get like this at times is a strength because we can see it. And then we can stand against it. That is being strong. But it doesn't mean it won't happen again. It will, because it does, in all of us. But now we know what we're dealing with.

This book takes up our need to see where we go wrong and get things wrong, so that we can choose to not be like we see we are being. The quotes help us to understand this, and they work with ways to do things and decide things, including choosing again and again to have a kinder heart.

This brings us to God, who gets a big part in the action. God is the whole source of life, and God is always wishing us well and giving what is good. When we choose not to stay in a wrong but turn from it, we are drawing from God's strength, which becomes the source of our strength.

That changes a lot of things for us because now we're not doing it all on our own.

Think about doing wrong. What is it that makes something wrong? Most people don't go around deliberately doing wrong, although of course some do. But there are other ways we can get into wrong – being judgmental about someone, or putting someone down, or just blaming them.

These attitudes go on in our private thoughts. We might not spot them, but when we look at how we think about other people, we can begin to see that we do have such views. We often react rather than respond.

What we often do is to try harder and hope we are getting better. But that way means we haven't dealt with the cause, which is some kind of wrong in us. And nobody is perfect!

Seeing our wrong doesn't mean we're bad or evil. It simply means we are human.

This book helps with how we can see that and how we can turn away each time.

The second part is that we choose to have a kinder heart, and we keep on choosing that. Think about that for a moment. What is being kind? What sort of thoughts come up? And why do we use the idea of a 'heart' to describe feelings?

A big question to ask ourselves is what changes choosing a kinder heart would bring about in us? What sort of changes?

This is what this book is about. It's personal but it's not about blaming ourselves or finding fault.

Doing personal work is something we just keep doing. As we do, it begins to work in us and help us to know ourselves more. We start feeling that we are getting stronger, steadier, finding our spiritual strength. That is incredibly good. It's a great gift from God when we start to make real decisions.

The quotes often mention God. God wants us to turn from our wrongs and choose a kinder heart. Whatever you believe about God, draw on the great help that a source of wisdom more than just our own brings us.

• • o O o • •

the QUOTES

We must look into ourselves

We must start seeing our personal states of mind in our thoughts and feelings, good or not, kind or unkind. This is a big change for us, but it opens up a new level in us where we see we do have faults and we can start managing them.

> Do you want to be saved? Then you must admit to your wrongdoing and do the work of being sorry for it.
>
> *Admitting our wrongdoing* means recognising the things we are doing that are destructive, seeing them in ourselves, admitting them, taking responsibility for them, and criticising ourselves for them. When we do this in front of God, we are admitting our wrongdoing.
>
> *Doing the work of being sorry for it* means, after admitting our wrongs, asking with a humble heart for help in giving them up, not doing them anymore, and living a new life in harmony with the principles of kindness and faith.

Take some time to look back at your own thoughts and feelings over recent days and see when it's been lovely, calm, and enjoyable and when it's been hard, strange, or upsetting in some way.

• • ○ ○ ○ • •

We must look closely

This passage tells us that instead of saying "nobody's perfect" (which is true) we need to be more specific about our faults. By doing this, we will see them and regret them, which is our starting point for dealing with them in a better way.

> **If we only admit in a general way that we are bad people, and consider ourselves guilty of all evil, but don't look closely at ourselves and identify our own wrongs, that _is_ making an admission, but it isn't an admission that makes us sorry for our wrongdoing. If we are unaware of the wrongs we are doing, we will keep living the same way we did before.**

Think about what you typically feel, think and do when you get upset. What helps you cope, and does it work or not?

· ● ○ ○ ○ ● ·

... If we are unaware of the wrongs we are doing, we will keep living the same way we did before ...

Here, we are being urged to look honestly at our intentions when we're involved in life and being with others close to us. We should do this while freeing our mind of things that stop us being ourselves, such as rules or laws or what people might think of us.

> **To look closely at ourselves so that we can do the work of being sorry for our wrongs, we must pay attention to our thoughts, and to the motives that drive us. We must think especially about what we would do if it were allowed, and if we weren't worried about the law and about damaging our reputation, status, and wallet. That's where we will find the faults in our character. That's where the damaging things we do with our body come from. If we don't explore the wrongs in our thinking and motives, we can't possibly do the work of being sorry for them because we will keep right on thinking and wanting what we did before. And wanting what is wrong is doing it. This is what it means to look closely at ourselves.**

Can you think of one thing about yourself that you would ideally like to be without?

• • o O o • •

We must look regularly

One important point about looking into ourselves is doing it quite often, even daily, but not all the time. This helps us see our own patterns and pitfalls, and find how God, who knows us completely, always sets us back up when we open ourselves to God.

> Living a life of kindness and faith means doing the work of being sorry for our wrongs every day, paying attention to the faults in our character, admitting them, not acting on them, and asking God for help.
>
> On our own we are always going downhill. But God is always lifting us up and leading us toward what is good. This is how it always works if we are focused on good things.
>
> But if we are focused on bad things we are always going downhill, and God is always lifting us up also, but God can only hold us back from stumbling into things that are even more destructive, which is what we always tend to do when we are on our own.

While it might feel strange to begin with, imagine talking with God and what might come up in your conversation.

• • ○ ○ ○ • •

... God is always lifting us up and leading us towards what is good ... if we are focused on bad things we are always going downhill, and God is always lifting us up also ... page 11

We need to live out our wish to change

This brings in a new point, that while we need to see and know ourselves, we must put what we discover into the way we live, and make changes. To work with God who always feels for us, we need to live by what God asks us to be like, and then things will start changing.

> Just *saying* that we're sorry but not *living* like we are is not doing the work of being sorry for our wrongs.

We don't give up our wrongdoing by *saying* we're sorry about it, but by *living* like we're sorry about it. God is always forgiving us for our faults, because God is pure mercy. But they stick to us even when we think we've given them up. The only way we can get rid of them is to live by the principles of truth that come from our beliefs. The more we live by these, the more our wrongs are pushed aside, and the more they are pushed aside, the more we give them up.

Choose some part of your life and find one way you can bring a change to it.

• • ○ ○ ○ • •

Tangible signs of us changing

While it is good to understand what's involved in seeing, accepting, and turning from our faults, it's also important to see changes in ourselves happening as a result. This passage gives us some examples.

> Here are some indications that we have given up our wrongs, meaning they have been pushed to the side:
>
> We enjoy praying to God for God's own sake, and we enjoy doing useful things for other people for their own sake. In other words, we enjoy doing good just because it is good, and speaking the truth just because it is true. We have no desire to take credit for our kindness and faith. We turn away from and reject wrongs such as unfriendliness, hatred, revenge, and adultery. We avoid even thinking about these kinds of things from any intention to do them.

As well as seeing if what is said here applies to you, can you think of two other changes that you've noticed in yourself as a result of turning from your own faults?

• • o O o • •

To help us get the whole picture, Swedenborg makes a list of signs that there hasn't been any change. This is not the same as those likely moments of personal weakness; the ones here are showing that there hasn't been any real intention of turning away from any of our faults.

> **But here are some indications that we have not given up our wrongs, and they have not been pushed to the side:**
>
> **We do not pray to God for God's own sake, or do useful things for other people for their own sake, and we do not do what is good and speak the truth for their own sake, but for our own sake and to gain material benefits for ourselves. We want to take credit for everything we do. We feel nothing unpleasant in wrongs such as unfriendliness, hatred, revenge, and adultery. We think about these things and base our opinions on them as much as we want to.**

It is possible for someone to live a spiritual life outwardly but not seem to be affected by it inwardly. Can you come up with any reasons why a person might keep up an outward spiritual life if there is no feeling for it inside them?

● ● ○ ○ ○ ● ●

Another important point brought out here is that as we make progress in turning from our faults, they seem to have gone from us. While it looks like this, the fact is that they have been pushed to the side by God and we are now being kept apart from them.

> **Some people think that when God forgives our wrongs they are completely wiped away, or dissolved like dirt washed away in water. But they are not washed away. They are only pushed to the side. Specifically, we are held back from them when God keeps us focused on what is good. When we are kept busy with good things, it feels to us like our wrongs are gone—as if they have been completely wiped away. And the more we can be kept focused on good things, the more our character is reshaped. If you think you can give up your wrongdoing in any other way, you are sadly mistaken.**

Do you think it is helpful to occasionally recall things you used to feel and do quite a long time ago? If not, why? If yes, why?

Changing freely as against being compelled

Here, we are shown how our freedom is so important in any new spiritual direction we take. We must want to take this up ourselves and feel free to, and not feel obliged or compelled.

> **If we do the work of being sorry for our wrongs in a state of freedom, it accomplishes something. But if we do it under compulsion, it doesn't accomplish anything. We are under compulsion when we are very sick, when we are depressed because of bad luck, when we are about to die, and when we are so scared that we can't think rationally. When bad people are under this type of pressure they may promise to stop doing bad things. They may even do some good things. But when they are free again they go right back to their old ways. It is different for good people.**

Think about freedom itself for a while and its value for us. What are some other parts of your life where having real freedom is so important for you?

• • o O o • •

We need to keep this whole process going

In anything new, it is easy to start and less easy to maintain it, for all sorts of reasons. Here, we are helped to take turning from our faults seriously and to stay in it even though we may find difficulties.

> **After we have looked closely at ourselves, recognized our wrongs, and done the work of being sorry for them, we should remain steady in a good life all the way to the end of our life. If we relapse into our old bad habits and take them up again, we become corrupt. Right and wrong get all mixed together in our life, making our character even worse than before. This is what Jesus was talking about when he said:**

'When an evil spirit leaves someone it travels through parched places, looking for rest but not finding it. Then it says, "I will return to my home, where I came from." When it returns, it finds the place empty, swept clean, and furnished. Then it goes and gets seven more spirits worse than itself and they go in and live there, and the person ends up worse off than before.' (Matthew 12:43–45)

What attainable ways can you come up with to help you strengthen your wish to keep your new direction going and happening?

• • ○ ○ ○ • •

The real purpose of religion

Knowing lots of religious ideas and teachings won't change our heart or make us wise. Only turning from evil will do that. While it is important to know religious ideas and teachings, this is to show us how and how not to be in our heart and life.

> Let's say we have an encyclopedic knowledge of all the intricacies of our church's doctrines, and we can support them both biblically and rationally. We know the doctrines of all the churches going many centuries back, and the doctrinal statements issued by all the church councils. We even know the truth, so that we can see and understand these doctrines. For example, we know what faith and charity are, we know what piety is, we know what repentance and the forgiveness of sins are, we know all about being born again, baptism, the Holy Supper, Jesus, redemption, and salvation.

All this—and yet if we do not avoid wrongdoing because it is wrong, we are not wise. It is all mere information without any life in it. That's because it is just an intellectual thing. It has nothing to do with the motives

... It is all mere information without any life in it. That's because it is just an intellectual thing. It has nothing to do with the motives that drive us ...

that drive us. Mere intellectual knowledge fades away over time, and after death we will toss out anything that is not in harmony with whatever love drives us.

Still, it is all-important for us to gain knowledge. That's what teaches us how we should live. And if we do live by it, then and not before our knowledge comes to life in us. "

Think of something that you have come to know that has been very helpful to you in managing your life.

• • o O o • •

Religion can seem separate from life, but this is not so. It's all about our life now. Our love and life are critically important because they form the basis for our life after we die.

> **Religion always applies to our life because after death each one of us *is* our own life. We remain just the same as we were in the world. We don't change at all. A bad life cannot be changed into a good one, and a good life cannot be changed into a bad one. They are opposites, and when opposites are brought together they annihilate each other. Since they are opposites, a good life is called 'life,' but a bad life is called 'death.'**

You can see, then, that religion always applies to our life. A religious life means doing what is good.

Can you come up with any connections between religion and ordinary everyday life?

• • ○ ○ ○ • •

... After death each one of us is our own life. We don't change at all. A bad life cannot be changed into a good one ...

Our first real need is to be aware of God, and from this turn away from our own wrong ideas and feelings. After this, our second real need is to go on and do what we know is good.

66 When we focus on God, avoid doing wrong because it is wrong, and do the work of our job or position sincerely, rightly, and faithfully, we become manifestations of kindness. This follows from the principle that we are born to become embodiments of kindness, and we cannot become embodiments of kindness unless we are always doing good deeds of useful service out of the joy of friendliness. When we do the work of our job or position sincerely, rightly, and faithfully out of the joy of friendliness, we are continually engaged in the good of service not only toward the community and the general public, but also toward specific people in the private sphere.

However, we can't do this unless we focus on God and avoid doing wrong because it is wrong. This is because the first priority in kindness is focusing on God and avoiding wrongdoing because it is wrong, and the second priority of kindness is doing good deeds. The good things we do are the good deeds of useful service that we engage in every day. Even when we are not doing them, we are thinking about doing them. There is an inner friendliness that dwells within us and wants to engage in good deeds.

In this way, we are always taking part in the kindness of being useful from morning to night, year after year, from youth to old age. There is no other way we can be a manifestation of kindness, meaning a vessel for kindness.

Can you see how these two needs and the order in which they come can build up in us a growing pattern of usefulness and kindness that we are receiving from God?

• • ○ ○ ○ • •

*... Our first priority in kindness
is focusing on God and avoiding
wrongdoing because it is wrong.
Our second priority of kindness
is doing good deeds ...*

We are born to become truly kind

We can grow in kindness only if we keep on being kind to others, always from a feeling for and a delight in kindness itself.

" **We are born to become embodiments of kindness. And we cannot become embodiments of kindness unless we are always doing good deeds of useful service for the people around us, out of the joy of friendliness.** "

Have a think about what's involved in keeping on being kind to other people. What do you think is really being required of us?

●　●　○　○　○　●　●

Our angelic and demonic influencers

A key truth is that within ourselves we are in connection with some spiritual community, either heavenly if we love what is good, or hellish if we love what is bad. We are unaware of this, but it is how it is, and it is for us to decide if we will stay in a hellish community or break away from its hold over us.

> **The spirit of each one of us is in some community. It is in community in heaven if we love what is good, and in a community of hell if we desire what is evil. We are not aware of this during our life in the world, and yet in spirit we are indeed in some community. Otherwise we would not even be alive. This is also how God manages us.**
>
> **If we are in a community of hell, God can guide us out of it only through the laws of divine providence that God has established. One of these is that we must realize that we are in hell and want to get out of it, and make an *effort* to get out as if we were doing it on our own. We can do this during our time on earth, but not after we die. After we die, we stay forever in the community that we placed ourselves in during our earthly lifetime.**

*... One of these laws of God is that
we must realise we are in hell and
want to get out of it ...*

This is why we should look at ourselves closely, see and recognize what is wrong with ourselves, and do the work of giving it up—and continue on this path for the rest of our life. "

One very helpful and revealing thing is for us to become aware of a thought and see its quality and whether it is kind or unkind, thoughtful or thoughtless. Try this out.

• • o O o • •

We either turn ourselves toward good or toward evil

Good and evil cannot coexist. Each one will drive out the other. This is true in our experience after we die and it is true in each moment of our life now.

> **Evil and good cannot coexist. As much as we set aside evil, we can see and sense what is good.**
>
> **Why? Because in the spiritual world people are surrounded by auras that reflect what they love. This aura spreads out all around them, touches other people, and causes harmony or friction with them. These auras separate good and bad people from each other.**
>
> **We must set aside what is bad before we can experience, feel, and love what is good. There are many material-world examples that support this. For example, we cannot visit someone who keeps leopards and panthers at home as pets. That person may be safe because that's who feeds them, but we can't visit until they are not in the house anymore.**

Think about what you are attracted to or feel drawn to and find a few examples. Being attracted to things makes us feel we are moving towards them. How do you experience that?

• • ○ ○ ○ • •

Each of us is what we love and how we live

What we love will come out into what we do and how we live. This flow is inbuilt even though life happening around us can look like random movement and activity.

> **Each one of us is our own love. Our love and our life work together and are one and the same. Our faith is the *character* of our love or life. And our faith goes hand-in-hand with our actions. The things we do embody everything we love and our entire life, since our actions are expressions and outcomes of them. They are the end result, in which everything before them comes together.**
>
> **This is why angels from the third heaven know people's character from their tone of voice, their gait, a touch of their hand, a physical gesture, their excitement, and from many other things they do. People on earth are not aware that all these things show our character to angels from the third heaven because people think they are just motions, and nothing more. And yet, the life of our mind brings them into being through the life of our body. Both of these centres of life in us, and our entire character, work together to bring them into being. In short, our character is expressed in our actions.**
>
> **Our actions include everything we do, say, and write, whether it's a lot or a little. For example, what managers do in their job, what clergy do in their job, what merchants do in their job, and what labourers do in their job.**

*...The things we do embody
everything we love and our entire
life, since our actions are expressions
and outcomes of them....*

Think about what you love being, feeling and thinking and
how this can get fulfilled in your outward life.

• • ○ ○ ○ • •

We are well able to turn from wrong

We can tell ourselves we are born with a wounded nature that we can't do anything about. This is simply not true. We are born with God's gift of freedom to turn our life either to this way or to that way.

> Many people believe in their heart that no one can avoid doing wrong from their own power because we are born in sin, and we have no power to avoid it. What these people need to know is that we can avoid doing wrong if we believe in our heart that there is a God, that Jesus is the God of heaven and earth, that the Bible comes from God, which makes it sacred, that there is a heaven and a hell, and that there is life after death.

This is not possible for people who think these things are silly, rejecting them in their minds, and especially for people who flatly deny them. If we never think about God, how can we think that this or that is an offence against God? If we never think about heaven, hell, and life after death, how can we avoid doing wrong because it is wrong? When we think like that, we do not know right from wrong.

We are positioned between heaven and hell. Heaven always influences us toward good, and hell always influences us toward evil. Since we are centred between the two of them, we have freedom to think well or to think badly.

God never takes this freedom away from us because it is our life, and makes it possible for us to reshape our character. As much as we use this freedom to think well, avoid doing wrong because it is wrong, and pray to God for help, God pushes our wrongdoing aside, and gives us the ability to restrain ourselves from acting on it as if we were doing it on our own, and in this way to avoid doing wrong. "

Do you feel there is anything in your own make-up that you are just stuck with? If so, would you be able to lessen its hold on you?

* * o O o * *

... God never takes this freedom away from us, because it is our life, and makes it possible for us to reshape our character ...

Our inner life needs thorough searching

It seems normal to us to look at our outward life and assess our faults and successes on that level. But because our intentions are the origin of our desires, we must look into that inner and more private level.

> We have an inner self and an outer self. Both of them must be reshaped for our character to be reshaped. And our character cannot be reshaped unless we look closely at ourselves, see and recognize our wrongs, and stop acting on them. We can't just pay attention to our outer self. We must pay attention to our inner self as well. If we pay attention only to our outer self, we see only what we have actually done. We see, for example, that we have not killed anyone, we have not been unfaithful to our partner, we have not stolen anything, we have not given false testimony, and so on. We are scrutinizing our physical wrongdoing, but not the wrongs in our spirit.

But to reshape our character we must pay attention to the wrongs in our spirit. After all, we live as spirits after death, which means that every wrong in our spirit stays with us. The only way to scrutinize our spirit is to pay attention to our thoughts, and especially to our intentions, since our intentions are what we are thinking about based on our motivation. This is the source and root of our wrongdoing: our desires and the pleasures that go with them. Unless we see and recognize these, we are still engaged in our wrongs even if we don't act on them outwardly. Thinking and intending is wanting and doing, as is clear from Jesus' words, *'Anyone who looks at someone else's wife with sexual desire for her has already committed adultery with her in his heart.'* **(Matthew 5:28)**

Do you feel that looking at our intentions is possible, is essential, is helpful, or is too hard?

. . o O o . .

... Our intentions are what we are thinking about based on our motivation ...

Wrongs can't go unless we can see them

It is important for us to see our wrongs. We can only
deal with, that is, see, choose, accept or reject what we have
seen ourselves doing, as otherwise we are just unaware of its
hold over us.

> We can't get rid of our wrongdoing unless it comes into
> view. This does not mean we should do bad things so that
> we can see them. It means that we should look closely at
> ourselves, and not only at what we do, but also at what we
> think about, and at what we *would* do if we weren't afraid
> of the law and of damaging our reputation. We should
> especially pay attention to what wrongs we inwardly think
> of as allowable, and do not think of as wrong. When that is
> our view of them, we are still doing them.

To make it possible for us to look closely at ourselves, we
are given a thinking mind distinct from our motivation.
This is so that we can know, understand, and recognize
what is good and what is bad, and based on this recognize
the character of our motives, meaning what we love and
desire. For this purpose, our thinking mind has been
given higher and lower levels of thought, which are also
inner and outer levels of thought. From the perspective of
our higher or inner thinking, we can see what our motives
are doing in our lower or outer thinking. It is like looking
at our face in a mirror.

When we see this, and know what is wrong with ourselves, if we then ask God for help we can stop wanting it, avoid it, and then act in the opposite way. Even if we can't do this freely, we can still force ourselves to do it through inner battles, and finally come to hate and despise our wrongs. Then and not before is when we first sense and feel that evil is evil and good is good.

This is what it means to look closely at ourselves, see what's wrong with ourselves, recognize it, admit it, and quit it. "

Have you ever had your eyes opened about something about you and inside you that you never realised was there? How helpful has it been for you? Was that realisation stressful or a relief?

● ● ○ ○ ○ ● ●

We must open the door of our heart

Selfish living closes our door to God, but turning from our self-interest toward God's inflowing life and its goodness opens our door. Then we can know, feel, and acknowledge God.

" Anyone can see based on common sense that destructive desires and their pleasures block off and close the door to God, and that God cannot evict those desires from us as long as we keep the door firmly shut, pushing and shoving against it from the other side to keep God from opening it. Wasn't it Jesus who said in the book of Revelation that we are the ones who must open the door?

'See, I am standing at the door knocking. If you hear my voice and open the door, I will come in to you and share a meal with you, and you with me.' (Revelation 3:20)

This makes it clear that as much as we avoid doing wrong because it is from the Devil and creates an obstacle preventing God from coming in, God will be bound to us more and more closely. This connection will be especially close if we loathe doing bad things as if they were fiery pitch-black devils—since evil and the Devil are the same thing, and the deceptions of evil are the same thing as Satan.

God flows into our love for what is good and into our attraction to it. In the process, God also flows into our related thoughts and ideas, all of which are true because they come from what is good.

In the very same way, the Devil, meaning hell, is within our love for what is evil and our attraction to it, which is mere craving. In the process, the Devil also flows into our related thoughts and ideas, all of which are false because they come from what is evil. "

What do you think is the main difference between heaven and hell in their tactics with us?

• • ○ ○ ○ • •

... Wasn't it Jesus who said in the book of Revelation that we are the ones who must open the door? ...

... I am standing at the door knocking. If you hear my voice and open the door, I will come in to you ... page 36

We must make choices by ourselves

The way God works with us is to give everything to us, but we have to feel it is all our own. This is important for us because we think and consider things, unlike animals. We are aware of ourselves, able to think about life and death, right and wrong. If it wasn't like this, we would not feel free and we would not be truly human. As a result, we choose the meaning, loves, and values of our life.

> If it did not seem to us as if we lived on our own, meaning that we think, are motivated, speak, and act on our own, we would not be human. This means that unless we managed our life and our work as if we were doing it based on our own good judgment, we could not be guided and managed by divine providence. We would be like people standing there with dangling hands, open mouths, closed eyes, and bated breath, just waiting for inspiration. In short, we would strip ourselves of our humanity, which comes from our feeling and sensation that we live, think, are motivated, speak, and act as if it

... Unless we managed our life and our work as if we were doing it based on our own good judgment, we could not be guided and managed by divine providence ...

were by ourselves. We would also strip ourselves of
the two capabilities that differentiate us from animals:
freedom and rationality. Without that sense of autonomy,
we would have no ability to receive and give in return,
which would take away our ability to live forever. "

Go and be quiet somewhere where you won't be interrupted
and just let the thought take flight that everything is given to
you by God but it feels to you that it is all your very own.

• ● ○ O ○ ● •

We must use our own judgment

It is up to us to use our own judgment whether we keep living by loving ourselves more than anything else or whether we will break free of that and ask God to lead our life. The first holds our door tightly shut; the second opens our door.

If you want to be led by divine providence, use your good judgment, like a labourer or manager who faithfully takes care of the boss's affairs. Our human good judgment is the money that was given to the servants to trade with in Luke 19:12–26 and Matthew 25:14–30, for which they were required to provide an accounting.

It appears to us as if this good judgment belonged to us. And it will continue to appear that way to us as long as we harbour within us the greatest enemy of God and divine providence, which is self-centred love. That kind of love takes up residence within each one of us from birth. If we do not recognize it—and it does not want to be recognized—it remains secure, and guards the door to prevent us from opening it so that God could evict that love from within us.

… If you want to be led by divine providence, use your good judgment, like a labourer or manager who faithfully takes care of the boss's affairs …

We do open the door when we avoid doing wrong because it is wrong as if we were doing this by ourselves, while recognizing that our ability to do so comes from God. This is the kind of good judgment that divine providence can work with. "

Look back and think of some of the important big personal choices you've had to make, and recall what you did finally choose, and perhaps why.

• • ○ ○ ○ • •

The true spiritual quality of our being never changes suddenly from being like this to now being like that. The reality is and must be that we are gradually transformed and re-made.

>   Life can't be breathed into us in an instant. It must be shaped step by step, and reshaped as we avoid doing wrong because it is wrong. We must know what is wrong, recognize it, admit it, and restrain ourselves from acting on it because we do not want it. We also must learn the ways that lead to an understanding of God.

These are the things that shape and reshape our life—and they can't be poured into us all at once. We must first push aside wrongs we are born into, and in their place plant good things that have heaven within them.

Based on the wrongs we are born into, we are like tar in our thinking and venom in our motives. But when our character has been reshaped, we are like clear water in our thinking and olive oil in our motives. Having our

... These are the things that shape and reshape our life – and they can't be poured into us all at once. We must first push aside wrongs we are born into ...

character transformed instantaneously would be like transforming tar into clear water or venom into olive oil. What person who knows anything at all about human life doesn't realize that this is impossible unless the qualities of the tar and the venom are taken away, and replaced with the qualities of the clear water and the olive oil? "

When we appreciate and act on each deepening moment, God will give us a sense of making progress in ourselves. Have you found that this happens?

We continue living as we are after death

All kinds of ideas abound about how we will live after we die. The simple fact is that we will live what we are choosing to love.

> People may have doubts about divine providence because up to now we have not known that people live as people after death, and this has not been revealed sooner. The reason we have not known this is that within people who do not avoid doing wrong because it is wrong there is a secret belief that there is no life after death. It wouldn't really matter if you told them that we live as people after death or that we are resurrected on Judgment Day. Even if some people do happen to believe in the afterlife, they say to themselves, 'It will not be any worse for me than it is for anyone else. If I go to hell, I will have plenty of company, just as much as if I go to heaven.'
>
> Still, anyone who has any religion at all has an instinctive belief that we live as people after death. The only people who think we live as ghosts and not as people are the ones who are all wrapped up in their own brilliance.

Search online something like "Ideas about an afterlife" and see the range of beliefs and outlooks.

• • ○ ○ ○ • •

It's essential for us to turn from wrong

It is essential because what we allow, take up with and make ours will become our life's love. Inevitably then, after we die, we will seek to fulfil this deeply embedded practised love.

> There's no need to explain that for us to reshape our character, we must be guided away from our wrongs. That's because if we are engaged in wrongdoing here on earth, we will be the same way after we leave this earth. If we don't do away with our wrongdoing on earth, we can't get rid of it later, either. Wherever a tree falls, that's where it lies. In the same way, whatever our life is like when we die, that's how it will stay.
>
> Also, we are judged by what we have done. It's not that everything we have done is put on a big list, but that we go back to doing the same kind of things we did before. Death, you see, is only a continuation of our life. The only difference is that after we die we can no longer reshape our character.

Try to find five words or phrases that express your deepest personal love. Look at each one in turn and arrange them in order of their intensity and power for you personally.

• • ○ ○ ○ • •

Turning from wrongs brings God

The result of us turning away from our faults because they go against God is that God can then bring us into a new and heavenly state of being. In fact we are like an angel in heaven.

" As much as we avoid and reject wrongdoing because it is wrong, and think about heaven, salvation, and eternal life, God adopts us and connects us to heaven. God also gives us a spiritual disposition that makes us not only want to know the truth, but understand it, and also be motivated by it and act on it.

This is how God reshapes our character. And as much as we continue to know and understand the truth, and be motivated by it and act on it, we become a new person, meaning a reborn person. We also become angels of heaven who have a heavenly love and life. "

Let your thought explore the logic that if something is filling something, nothing else can come in unless it is removed, then other things can come in. Then look at this personally.

Turning from wrongs brings the opposite

There is a clear spiritual law that when we turn from a wrong because it is wrong, we come into its opposite good. This is how it is with each specific wrong there is.

> Bad and good are opposites, just as hell and heaven are opposites, or the Devil and God. This means that if we avoid doing bad things because they are bad, we arrive at the opposite of what is bad. The good thing that is opposite to the bad thing meant by 'murder' is the virtue of loving our neighbour.
>
> Since this good and that bad are opposites, if we engage in the bad, it pushes out the good. Opposites cannot be together, just as heaven and hell cannot be together. If they are, they become lukewarm, as described in the book of Revelation:
>
> *'I know that you are neither cold nor hot. I wish you were either cold or hot. But since you are lukewarm, and neither cold nor hot, I will spit you out of my mouth.'*
> (Revelation 3:15–16)

Do you feel it is just as true to say that if we turned from a good love we would then come into its opposite wrongness?

• • ○ ○ ○ • •

Change happens when we turn from wrongs

Experiencing change in ourselves is important for us to discover. There is no empty nothingness in spiritual things – if we turn away from some wrong, the opposite of it will start to be seen and felt.

> **The battle is not hard unless we have allowed our wrong desires to break free, and intentionally engaged in them. It is also hard for people who have stubbornly rejected the sacred things in the Bible and in the church. For other people, though, it is not hard. Even if you beat back your bad motives just once a week or twice a month, you will notice a difference.**

The best thing you can do with this idea is to try it out in the way that you feel is best for you.

● ● o O o ● ●

Hating wrongness brings God's rightness

In ourselves we are not virtuous but when from ourselves we turn away from deceit, trickery, and other wrongs, then God can give us a love for integrity.

> **Honesty also means integrity, fairness, faithfulness, and right action. On our own we cannot be engaged in these virtues based on the virtues themselves and for their own sake. But if we turn away from fraud, swindling, and cheating because it is wrong, we are engaged in those virtues not from ourselves, but from God. This applies to us no matter what our job or career might be: pastor, government official, judge, merchant, or labourer.**

Think about the kind of thoughts someone might well have when they make a firm decision to avoid something like deception and seek openness and honesty.

· · ○ ○ ○ · ·

Hating wrongs leads to doing good

People who hate what is wrong see the value of doing what is good. People who believe that good is from God will see this even more clearly. People who have mere faith in God won't see it at all.

> **Talk to any ordinary people you want to, whether they are domestic workers, farmers, manual labourers, sailors, or shopkeepers—assuming they have some common sense—and tell them that anyone who hates doing wrong will do what is good, and they will see it clearly. The ones who know that everything good comes from God will see, if you say it to them, that as much as people hate doing wrong because it is against God's will, they will do what is good from God.**
>
> **But say the same thing to people who have convinced themselves that faith alone saves, and that no one can do anything good on their own, and they will not see it. That's because the false beliefs they have adopted have closed off their thinking mind. It is different for ordinary people.**

Have a think and see if you are horrified by any wrongs that are done. Does hearing about dreadful wrongs make you want to do what is good all the more? What do you think is meant by "People who have a mere faith in God won't see it at all"?

• • ○ ○ ○ • •

When we turn from wrongs, we will then do what is good

People can know what is evil but justify doing it themselves. Only when we turn from our wrongs because they are wrong are we able to do true and genuine good that comes from a belief or a higher motive, and that proceeds from the intention of our heart.

> There are judges who live a religious life, and yet do not think it is a religious offence to render judgment based on friendship and connections, with an eye to wealth and prestige. Even if they are aware that these are offences, they convince themselves that they are not wrong. It's the same for people in other professions.
>
> Avoiding wrongdoing because it is wrong and doing spiritual good are not the same. If we avoid doing wrong because it is wrong, we will do spiritual good. But if we do good without avoiding wrongdoing because it is wrong, none of the good we do is *spiritual* good. That's because doing wrong is at cross-purposes with kindness. That's why we must first stop doing wrong. Only then can we do good deeds from kindness, meaning from a kind heart. We cannot do good as long as our desire is to do evil. We cannot desire both good and evil at the same time.
>
> Every good deed that is truly good flows from our inner motives. We get rid of our bad motives by being actively sorry for them.

*... If we do good without
avoiding wrongdoing because
it is wrong, none of the good we
do is spiritual good ...*

We are quite capable of justifying things that we do, say, think, or feel. Think about what is going on inside us when we justify ourselves. What else other than ourselves could we consider, and do you think these would go against our own justifications?

· · ○ ◯ ○ · ·

Hating wrongs clears the way

Practising the method of examining our intentions and seeing our thoughts can lead us to dislike and oppose the self-centred states we can be in. We now see that they come to us from hell and we need to relegate them back there.

> We look closely at our motives and intentions when we pay attention to what we are thinking about. Our intentions show themselves in our thoughts. For example, if we are thinking about, wanting, and intending revenge, marital unfaithfulness, theft, and false testimony, and we have a desire for them. Also if we curse God, the Holy Bible, and the church. And so on.
>
> If we focus on these thoughts and desires within ourselves, and consider whether we would act on them if we were not afraid of the law and of damaging our reputation, and then, after engaging in this sort of self-examination, decide that we do not want these things to be a part of ourselves because they are wrong, then we are doing the true and deep work of being sorry for our wrongs.
>
> This is especially so when we feel pleasure in these types of wrongs, and would be free to act on them, but we resist the urge, and do not do them. If we continue to do this over and over again, when the pleasure of that wrong comes back it will start feeling distasteful to us, so that in the end we send it packing to hell. This is what Jesus meant when he said, *'If you want to save your life, you will lose it. But if you lose your life for my sake, you will find it.'* (Matthew 10:39)

When we root out the wrongs in our intentions by doing this work of being sorry for them, we are like someone who gets to the weeds planted in the field by the Devil in time to pull them out, so that the seeds planted by God our Saviour can grow free and undisturbed in the soil, and produce their crop. (*see Matthew 13:24–30*)

Try detaching from a bad thought or an unkind feeling and after disowning it, send it to hell.

● ● ○ ○ ○ ● ●

... If we continue to resist over and over again, when the pleasure of that wrong comes back it will start feeling distasteful to us, so that in the end we send it packing to hell ...

The importance of being useful in some way

It is spiritually healthy for us to take part in some useful activity in life, and keep this principle happening. But we should keep the level of usefulness within our means and ability.

> **If we don't keep ourselves continually engaged in useful service, there is a break in the action. This dead time can get us side-tracked into other kinds of love and desire, not only putting our life of kindness on pause, but pulling us away from it. If this happens, our kindness dies because we have been taken over by its opposite. We are then serving two masters. (Matthew 6:24)**

Think about how doing something useful, maybe practical, for others, can bring a benefit to our own spiritual life and thought.

• • o O o • •

The absurdity of thinking God will do everything for us

We need to turn against our own wrongs and deal with them and not expect God to somehow do it all. This does not mean God does nothing. It means that as we deal with what we know about, God can then deal with the deeper wrongs in us.

> We should cleanse ourselves from wrongdoing, and not expect that God will do it for us in an instant. Otherwise we're like a farmhand whose face and clothes are covered with soot and manure, who goes to the supervisor and says, 'Boss, wash me!' Won't the boss say, 'What are you talking about, you fool? Look! There's water, soap, and a towel. Don't you have hands that you can use? *Wash yourself!'*
>
> In the very same way, God will say to us, 'I have given you what you need to cleanse yourself. I have also given you the motivation and the ability. Use these capabilities and gifts of mine as if they were yours, and you will be cleaned.' And so on. In the whole chapter of Matthew 23 Jesus taught that we should wash our outer self, but we should do it from our inner self.

Get an orange or mandarin. Look at it. What can you see? What can't you see? Why is there peel? Now peel it. What do you do with the peel? What do you do with the segments? Think about this illustration.

● ● ○ ○ ○ ●

Faith by itself without any good deeds is not enough

Putting everything to do with religion only into belief and not into doing what is good or turning from wrongs because they are wrong is missing the important point. We can only be truly religious when we are obeying what God commands us.

" These days people commonly think that salvation comes from believing this or that Christian teaching, and not from living by the Ten Commandments—meaning not murdering, being unfaithful, stealing, and giving false evidence, both in the strict sense of these things and in a broad sense. People say that salvation has nothing to do with our actions. It depends entirely on the faith God gives us, they say.

But let's be serious. If we're doing bad things, we have no faith.

Consider it logically. Can people who engage in murder, adultery, theft, and giving false testimony really have faith as long as their desire to do such things persists? And is there any way to get rid of that desire besides not wanting to do these things because they are wrong—meaning because they are hellish and diabolical?

Anyone who thinks that salvation comes from believing this or that Christian teaching but lives in the wrong way like that is nothing but a fool, as Jesus says in Matthew 7:26. The prophet Jeremiah paints a picture of churches that teaches this:

'Stand in the door of the Lord's house and make this proclamation: This is what the Lord of Armies, the God of Israel, says: Change your ways! Correct your behaviour! Do not trust those lying words, "This is the Temple of the Lord, the Temple of the Lord, the Temple of the Lord!" Will you steal, murder, commit adultery, and lie under oath, and then come and stand before me in this house, which has my name written on it, and say, "We are saved!" when you are doing all these horrendous things? Has this house become a hideout for criminals? Yes, I have seen it! says the Lord.' (Jeremiah 7:2–4, 9–11)

Can you come up with any ideas why some people emphasise that belief is the important thing and doing good is less so or even doesn't count?

• ● ○ ○ ○ ● •

Just thinking kind actions will save us ignores the state of our own heart

If we believe that doing good and being kind by itself saves us, we are mistaken because we haven't thought about our intentions. When we love doing good and being kind for their own sakes and because of God, then this saves us.

> **If we think that kindness is all about engaging in charitable acts and giving generously, but we are not kind people within ourselves, then we inwardly align ourselves with the residents of hell, and outwardly with the residents of heaven. However, after death our outward character is taken away. All that's left is our inner character.**

Our physical heart sends blood everywhere in us to feed everything. How does our 'heart' describe our best and deepest love?

• • o O o • •

*... after death our outward character is taken away.
All that's left is our inner character ... page 60*

Doing good without turning from our wrongs doesn't work

It's all too easy to do good things and think we are being kind yet at the same time we do not turn away from our own wrongs. The two together are part of the same process. Turning from our wrongs because they are wrong leads to us being genuinely kind.

> **We can do good deeds that we think of as kindness while not avoiding wrongdoing. However, wrongdoing is always at cross-purposes with kindness.**
>
> **It is obvious that avoiding wrongdoing and doing good are not the same thing. After all, there are people who do all sorts of good and kind things out of religious devotion and because they are thinking about eternal life, but who still don't think it is wrong to indulge in hatred and revenge, illicit sex, theft and property damage, slander and false testimony, and many other offences.**

Write down about 7 things that you do inside yourself, such as "planning, choosing, wanting" and add others, or do your own full list. Look at each of these activities, and consider how important it is to check that they are being done with kindness.

● ● ○ 〇 ○ ● ●

Not turning from wrongs means they stay

If we notice where we are doing what is wrong but we do not turn from it, we still have it in us. We are meant to be receivers of God's love and blessing but this will prevent us.

> Our wrongs remain within us just as much as we do not avoid doing wrong because it is wrong.

We humans were created in the image and likeness of God. We were also made to be vessels that can receive God's love and wisdom. However, because we did not want to be recipients, but wanted to be love and wisdom ourselves so that we would be like God, we changed character, turning our thoughts and feelings away from God and toward ourselves. We began to love and even worship ourselves more than God. As a result, we cut ourselves off from God, focusing our attention in the opposite direction. In doing so, we corrupted the image and likeness of God within ourselves, making it an image and likeness of hell instead.

This is the meaning of eating from the tree of knowledge of good and evil. The snake that we listened to represents

... Sensory life loves earthly things. If we allow it to run our life, it will draw our mind away from heavenly things ...

the life and desires of our physical senses, which are the lowest and most earthly part of a person. Since our sensory life is connected to this world and gets its sensations from it, it loves earthly things. If we allow it to run our life, it will draw our mind away from heavenly things, which are the good things that come from love together with the understanding of truth that goes with wisdom. Seen as they truly are, these are Godly things.

This is how our human sense of self came to consist of nothing but destructive desires, which we are born into from our parents.

Think about the following statement and what it is saying: "We are only loving when we are being loving".

• • ○ ○ ○ • •

Emphasising only faith by itself kills deeper searching

Faith by itself is believing that our sins (wrongs) have been taken away by the sacrifice made by Jesus. It claims that we can't do anything about our wrongness, that Jesus has solved this problem on our behalf, and we will be saved by believing it.

> I have often been amazed that even though the whole Christian world is aware that we must avoid doing evil things because they are sins, and that otherwise we are not forgiven, and that if our sins are not forgiven we are not saved, hardly one person in a thousand knows this.

I looked into it in the spiritual world and found that it's true. Even though Christians are aware of it from the prayers that are read to them when they take the Holy Supper, where this is stated very clearly, when they are asked whether they know this, they answer that they do not know it and they never have. That's because they have not thought about

... When people who have convinced themselves of salvation by faith alone read the Bible, they don't see anything it says about love, kindness, and good works ...

it. For many of them, it's because they have thought only about faith, and about salvation by faith alone.

I have also been amazed that faith alone has closed their eyes so tight that when people who have convinced themselves of faith alone read the Bible, they don't see anything it says about love, kindness, and good works. It's as if they have smeared 'faith' all over the whole Bible, like someone scribbling in red ink all over a manuscript, blocking out everything under it—and if anything does appear, it is drowned out by faith and called faith. "

Have you ever been asked if you are saved? If so, what did you say? If not, what would you want to say?

● ● o O o ● ●

... It's as if they have smeared 'faith' all over the whole Bible, like someone scribbling in red ink all over a manuscript, blocking out everything under it ... page 65

Just saying we do wrong changes nothing

It is easy for us to generally say we are sinners yet never focus on any one specific problem we have in us. Afterwards we might feel washed clean but we are no different than we were before.

> Some people confess that they are guilty of all sins, but do not look for any wrongs in themselves. They say, 'I am a sinner! I was born in sin! There is nothing sound in me from head to foot! I am nothing but evil! Dear God, be gracious to me! Forgive me! Purify me! Save me! Make me walk in purity, and on a just path!' and things like that. And yet, they do not look closely at themselves, and therefore do not see a single thing wrong with themselves.
>
> People can't avoid, still less fight against, what they do not even know about. These people think they are washed clean after making this kind of confession. The reality is that they are filthy dirty from head to foot. When we confess all sins, we are only putting ourselves to sleep about them, and in the end blinding ourselves.

Choose a particular wrong that we may do and think of some practical ways of correcting it.

● ● ○ ◯ ○ ● ●

No change if we aren't serious

It's easy for us to be casual about our faults and find ways of excusing them. Only seeing that they go against God and against good can make us want their hold on us to be broken.

> **Many people do not realize that they are embedded in evil because they do not do wrong things outwardly. But they don't do wrong things because they are afraid of civil law and of damaging their reputation. And so, by custom and practice they train themselves to avoid doing wrong because it would be harmful to their position in society and to their wallet.**
>
> **However, if we do not avoid doing wrong from spiritual principles, simply because they are wrong and against God, the desire for them continues to lie hidden within us, like tainted water that is dammed up and stagnant. Pay attention to your thoughts and the motives behind them, and you will find these wrongs—assuming you know right from wrong.**

Imagine you are explaining to someone about looking honestly into your own life, your own thoughts and reactions, and seeing some faults and weaknesses. How would you talk about this?

We can delude ourselves that we've changed

It is amazing that we can think we have changed when in fact we haven't done anything or chosen anything to bring on a real change. We have our faith in God that upholds us, and we know what a moral life means, but we haven't put them into the way we live our life.

> Many people have been taught that faith has nothing to do with good deeds, and have convinced themselves of this. Since they don't believe that the law will condemn them, they pay no attention to what's right and wrong. Some even doubt that they can do anything wrong, or think that if they do, it is not wrong in God's eyes because they have been pardoned.
>
> This is also how it is for people who derive ethics from natural law, believing that morality is based on the practicalities of life in human culture and society, and there is no such thing as divine providence.
>
> And this is how it is for people who carefully cultivate a reputation and name for honesty and fair-dealing in order to gain status or profit.
>
> However, after death people like this who also have a contempt for religion become embodiments of their inner desires. To themselves they seem to be human, but to others, from a distance they look like satyrs. Like nocturnal birds, they can see in the dark, but not in daylight.

... Since they don't believe that the law will condemn them, they pay no attention to what's right or wrong. Some even doubt that they can do anything wrong ...

Think of a situation in which a wrong feeling about something or someone can be a pleasant feeling, something we even enjoy.

● ● ○ ⵔ ○ ● ●

Claiming to have a belief in God

If we intentionally do wrong we can still believe in God and heaven and hell, but it's all just ideas and things we know. If we aren't turning away from our wrong because it goes against God, this belief is nothing and it can't sustain us.

> All our actions, whether big or small, are good when God is in them, but bad when they come from ourselves. They are also good as much as we avoid doing wrong as an offence against God, and bad when we do not avoid doing wrong.
>
> It is the same with our faith. The quality of our actions shows the quality of our faith. They work together like thinking and talking, and like motivation and action.
>
> People think they can have faith no matter how badly they live, if they at least believe that there is a God, that Jesus is the Saviour of the world, that there is a heaven and a hell, and that the Bible is holy. But I can assure you, if we don't avoid doing wrong because it is wrong, and if we don't then focus on God, we don't really believe these things, because they are not part of our life and our love. They are only bits of knowledge in our memory. They do not become part of our life and love until we have struggled against wrongdoing and overcome it.
>
> This has become very clear to me from seeing many people after death who thought they had at least believed there is a God, that Jesus is the Saviour of the world, and so on. But if they lived bad lives, they did not really believe these things.

Look at this statement by Jesus in Matthew 7:21-23, *"Not everyone who says to me 'Lord, Lord,' will enter the kingdom of heaven, but the one who does the will of my Father who is in heaven. On that day many will say to me, 'Lord, Lord, did we not prophesy in your name, and cast out demons in your name, and do many mighty works in your name?' And then I will declare to them, 'I never knew you; depart from me, you workers of lawlessness'."* What do you think Jesus means?

• • o O o • •

> *... They do not become part of
> our life and love until we have
> struggled against wrongdoing
> and overcome it ...*

When there is only outward piety

Being devoted to God must lead to us searching inside ourselves for what needs to change. If this is happening, our devotion is real; if it isn't, our devotion may well be just a pretence or a habit.

> If we think and speak virtuously but do not turn away from wrongdoing because it is wrong, our virtuous thoughts and words are not virtuous, because we are not in relationship with God.
>
> Let's say we go to church all the time, listen carefully to the sermon, read the Bible and religious books, take the Holy Supper, and pour out prayers every day so that we are always thinking about God and salvation—and yet we don't consider it important to avoid engaging in wrong and destructive things such as deception, being unfaithful to our partner, hatred, slander, and so on. Any virtuous things we think and say can't possibly be virtuous inwardly because our own ego and bad character are behind them. Even if we don't realize it, that's what is inwardly driving us, no matter how hidden it is from our awareness. It's like a spring whose water is polluted right from its source. Our virtuous practices are just a matter of habit, or to make us look good, or pure hypocrisy. Yes, they do float up toward heaven. But on the way there they get turned around and sink back down like smoke in the air.

What ways do you have of ritualising your spiritual life. Why does doing this matter to you?

• • ○ ○ ○ •

Outward piety and what happens after we die

This passage describes the outcome of purely external religion with no wish to change loves, attitudes and thoughts. After death such a person finds they go where their own heart will lead them.

> I have been allowed to see and hear many people in the afterlife who trotted out all their good works, their religious piety, and much more. I noticed that some of them were carrying lamps without oil. However, when an inquiry into their actions revealed that they had not turned away from wrongdoing because it is wrong, they were told that they were bad people. Later they were seen going into caves where the same type of bad people lived.

If you believe there is a God, what do you think God wants from you and for you to do?

· · o O o · ·

It's our fault if we aren't heavenly

Our eternal existence is based on two linked truths; one is that God's intention and work is to lead us to heaven. The other is that we must turn from our wrongs because they go against what God needs to lead us to heaven.

> After death, everyone is given what they need to live a better life, if that is possible. They are taught and led by God through angels. Since they now know that we do continue to live after death, and that there is a heaven and a hell, at first they accept the truth. But the ones who have not believed in God, and have not avoided doing wrong because it is wrong on earth, soon grow tired of the truth, and go away.
>
> People who believed with their mouth but not in their heart are like the foolish virgins who had lamps but no oil. They begged the others for oil, and even went and bought some, but they were still not allowed into the wedding. Lamps symbolize religious truth, and oil symbolizes the good of kindness.
>
> Based on this, we can be assured that under divine providence everyone can be saved. If we aren't saved, it is nobody's fault but our own.

What do you think of this statement, "Everything is given us by God, yet everything seems to be all mine"?

• • ○ ○ ○ • •

While it is true that we can't do good ourselves since all good is from God, we are to turn from any evil in us and ask God to help us. Then we can do good that is from God.

" It is true that we humans are not capable of doing good that is actually good from our own self. But it is outrageous to use this fact to tear down all the good things people do when they turn away from wrongdoing because it is wrong. It is an utter rejection of the Bible, which commands us to do good deeds. It is contrary to the teaching that we are to love God and our neighbour, which together are the linchpin of the Law and the Prophets. It undermines and marginalizes every religion, because everyone knows that religion is all about doing good, and that we will all be judged on that basis.

We humans are able to avoid wrong behaviour through God's power as if we were doing it ourselves, if we ask for the strength to do it. And when we have done this, everything good we do is from God. "

Choose five things that you feel are genuinely good, either outwardly in action or inwardly in your attitude and intention.

Overemphasising faith can leave goodness out

When a religion says it's our faith that puts us right with God, this often leaves out our responsibility to do what we know is good. When we do good, we're meant to appreciate that all good is from God, not from us. But we are still required to do what is good.

> **There are many people in the Christian Church who teach that we are saved by faith alone, and not at all by living a good life, meaning doing good deeds. They even insist that wrong ways of life and bad deeds do not condemn people who are justified by faith alone, because they are in God and are under God's grace.**

And yet it is remarkable that even though they teach things like this, they still recognize that people who live a good life are saved, while people who live a bad life are condemned. This recognition comes from a common human intuition that flows in from heaven. It is clear that they do recognize this from the prayer that is read to the people before the Holy Supper in the churches in England, Germany, Sweden, and Denmark. It is well-known that faith alone is taught in these countries. Here is the prayer that is read in England to the people who gather to take the Holy Supper:

'The way and means to be received as worthy partakers of that Holy Table, is First, to examine your lives and conversations by the rule of God's commandments,

and whereinsoever ye shall perceive yourselves to have offended either by will, word or deed, there to bewail your own sinfulness, and to confess yourselves to Almighty God, with full purpose of amendment of life; and if ye shall perceive your offences to be such as are not only against God, but also against your neighbours, then ye shall reconcile yourselves unto them, being ready to make restitution and satisfaction according to the utmost of your powers, for all injuries and wrongs done by you to any other, and being likewise ready to forgive others that have offended you, as ye would have forgiveness of your offences at God's hand, for otherwise the receiving of the Holy Communion doth nothing else but increase your damnation. Therefore if any of you be a blasphemer of God, or a hinderer or slanderer of His Word, or an adulterer, or be in malice or envy, or in any other grievous crime, repent you of your sins, or else come not to that Holy Table; lest after the taking of that Holy Sacrament the Devil enter into you, as he entered into Judas, and fill you full of all iniquities, and bring you to destruction both of body and soul.'

How would you describe the best way someone can do what is good?

• • ○ ○ ○ • •

When we turn from our wrongs we love being useful for its own sake

We can be unsure if we are being useful for its own sake or for our own gain or promotion. The one thing that will make it genuinely unselfish is to turn against any wrong impulses or thoughts in ourselves.

> When we love to do useful things for their own sake, we are not as clearly aware of it as we are when we love to do them for our own benefit. That's why when we are engaging in useful service we may not know whether we are doing it simply to be helpful or whether we are doing it to gain some benefit for ourselves.
>
> But please know that we are doing useful things for their own sake when we are avoiding wrongdoing. As much as we do avoid wrongdoing, we are not engaging in useful service for our own sake, but from God. After all, evil and good are opposites. This means that if we are *not* wrapped up in wrongdoing, then we *are* engaged in good. We can't be simultaneously engaged in evil and good, because no one can serve two masters at the same time.
>
> Perhaps we aren't sure whether we are doing useful things for the sake of the service itself or for our own benefit. Stated another way, perhaps we aren't sure whether our good deeds are spiritual or materialistic. But this is how we can tell the difference: do we or do we not think it is wrong to do things that are wrong? If we think it is wrong, and therefore avoid wrongdoing, then the useful things

we do are spiritual. And when we start to avoid wrongdoing because we find it offensive, that's when we begin to have a conscious feeling that we love to do useful things for their own sake, and from a sense of spiritual joy in doing them. 99

How do you understand the idea of "being useful for its own sake"? Describe what this means in a few words, then think about the feelings you might get when you do this. It may help to recall an experience of it.

• • ○ ○ ○ • •

*… This means that if we are not
wrapped up in wrongdoing, then
we are engaged in good …*

We are kind when we have the welfare of other people within us

Being kind is a beautiful part of our shared humanity. Being kind in our relationships, responsibilities, and those moments when kindness is called for, brings the heart of God's loving care into our daily living. We are kind to others; the kindness we give is good to us.

> **Charitable acts are all the good things we do in our free time, of our own free will, if we are embodiments of kindness. No one is saved because of these charitable acts. Rather, we are saved because of the kindness from which we do them. Charitable acts such as these are outside us, whereas kindness is within us. We are saved based on the type of good and kindness that we have inside us.**

Why do you think voluntary work is especially rewarding and appreciated?

· · o O o · ·

Kindness itself doesn't save, but why we are kind will

Doing good itself doesn't save us or bring heaven into us. The *reason* we do good is what brings heaven in us, in the love and deep feeling we have for goodness and also in our turning away from our own self-interest.

> After death, many people who had thought about their own salvation in the world, when they realize that they are still alive and hear that there is a heaven and a hell, make a great show of all the good deeds they have done, giving to the poor, helping underprivileged people, and making contributions to religious charities. But they are asked, 'What were your motives? Did you avoid wrongdoing because it is wrong? Did you even think about it?'

Some of them answer, 'I had faith.' But they are told, 'If you did not consider your own wrongdoing to be offences, it doesn't matter how much faith you had. Faith and wrongdoing don't mix.'

They are then asked how they had gone about their working life. Did they work their job only for reputation, status, and profit, seeing these as the main goal, so that they were mostly thinking about themselves? Or did they work their job for the benefit of other people? They answered that they didn't see any difference. They were then told, 'If you focused on God and avoided doing wrong because it is wrong, the difference would become obvious to you because God *does* see the difference.' Then they were told that if they had made no distinction between them, they were acting from evil and not from good.

In the spiritual world our temperament is clearly expressed. Everyone can see our character. And whatever our temperament is like, it is expressed in everything that flows from us. This is how we are guided to the community where our specific temperament reigns. "

What kind of attitude may well come about in us if we just do good to be seen to be doing good? What attitude may well develop when we do what is good for its own sake?

· · ○ ○ ○ · ·

Truth needs to be lived to come alive in us

Religious truth receives goodness into itself, but we must also turn from our wrongs or else these truths will be fruitless and cold.

> This is why we are saved if we are focused on spiritual truth, as long as we move away from things that are wrong:

Spiritual truth is like a bucket made to hold good things. And the bucket does hold good things as much as we move away from things that are wrong. That's because God is always pouring good things into our bucket, but if we are living a bad life, it blocks us from accepting those good things into the truth that we have learned and stored away in our memory. So as much as we move away from things that are wrong, good things enter into us and fill the space provided by the truth we know. Our spiritual truth then becomes spiritual good.

It is quite possible for us to know the truth and say we believe it from some materialistic motive. We can even convince ourselves that it is true. And yet the truth is not alive within us as long as we are living a bad life. We are like a tree that has only leaves, and no fruit. That kind of truth is like light that has no warmth in it. It is like the light of winter, when nothing grows. But when there is warmth in it, it becomes like the light of springtime, when everything starts to grow.

The Bible compares truth to light, and even calls it light. It also compares love to warmth, and calls it spiritual warmth.

In the other life, truth even expresses itself as light, and good expresses itself as warmth. But truth without good expresses itself as cold light, while truth together with good expresses itself as a springtime light. This makes it clear what spiritual truth is like when the good of kindness is missing. "

Do you enjoy knowing spiritual ideas and teachings? How would you describe your enjoyment about this when you are, say, talking with a friend?

• • ○ ○ ○ • •

... Spiritual truth is like a bucket made to hold good things. And the bucket does hold good things as much as we move away from things that are wrong ...

This passage gives a number of common situations in life where something has to be done or removed before the thing can be used or be ready. Many comparable examples bring out the common sense we need and have in life.

> **If we were invited to dinner with a dignitary, wouldn't we go and wash our hands and face first? Would we go to bed with our partner in marriage on our wedding night without first washing our whole body?**
>
> **Can we get pure gold and silver without refining the ores to separate them from the slag? Who wouldn't separate the weeds from the wheat during harvest before storing it in the barn? Who wouldn't thresh the heads of barley with a winnowing rod before gathering them into the house? Who wouldn't clean and cook raw meat to make it edible before putting it on the table? Who wouldn't shake the bugs off the leaves of the trees in an orchard to keep them from eating up the leaves and wrecking the fruit?**

Think of two practical things you would say are common sense. Then think of two spiritual things (in your attitude or response to someone) where you again need common sense.

· · ○ ○ ○ · ·

... Can we get pure gold and silver without refining the ores to separate them from the slag? ... page 87

All good and truth come from God

Although we live our own life and we can do good and think what is true, it is important for us to see and know that all of these are given to us from God.

66 God has provided a pathway for us to avoid the spiritual death that comes from our destructive desires. We must focus on God, recognizing that every good thing that comes from love and all our understanding of truth that goes with wisdom comes from God, and none of it from ourselves. This is how we can make our character right, turning away from ourselves and toward God. This is how we can return to the form in which we were created—which was as receivers of what is good and true from God, and not at all from ourselves.

Because we turned away from God, causing our sense of self to consist of nothing but destructive desires, there is another pathway to recover the image of God: avoiding wrongdoing because it is wrong. If we avoid doing wrong, not because it is wrong but because it causes problems for us, we are not really focusing on God. We are focusing on ourselves, which means our character will continue to be corrupt. However, when we avoid doing wrong because it is wrong, we avoid it because it puts us in opposition to God, and because it is against God's divine laws. Then, when we pray to God for help and for the strength to resist it—and prayers for strength are never rejected—we can be purified from the destructive desires that we are born into.

If we do not embrace these two pathways, the only possible outcome is that our inborn character will stay with us.

If we only focus on God and pray, we cannot be purified from our wrongs. Doing this leads us to believe that after we have prayed, we have no wrongs left in us because they have been banished. We think this means they have been washed away. However, they still maintain their grip on us. And as long as they do, our wrongs only grow stronger. There is a spectre of death within us that feeds on and kills everything around it.

We also cannot get rid of our wrongs only by avoiding them. If we try to do this, we are focusing on ourselves, which will only strengthen our original faulty character. This is what happens if we turn ourselves backwards, away from God and toward ourselves. ,,

What is the real value in living in and from the belief that everything is given to us from God?

• • o O o • •

God is everywhere in the design of everything

We are created in the design that God has for everything, so God is in us because God is that design. But that is true only as far as we follow that design in the way we live.

> **God is present everywhere. And wherever things are arranged the way God designed them, God is present as if in God's own self, since God is that arrangement. Because God is everywhere, we are in God just as much as we live in harmony with God's design.**
>
> **God is in us because we humans are created as an embodiment of the divine pattern. But God is in us only as much as we live in harmony with that pattern. If we don't live in harmony with it, God is still in us, but only in our highest levels. These are the levels of our mind that make it possible for us to understand and want what is good. After all, it is God's presence in us that gives us the ability to understand and the tendency to love.**

*... In heaven it is common wisdom
that God is in all people, both good ones
and bad ones, but that people are not in
God unless they live in harmony
with God's design ...*

As much as we do not live in harmony with the divine pattern, we close off the lower levels of our mind or spirit, preventing God from flowing down into them and filling them with God's presence. This means that God is in us, but we are not in God.

In heaven it is common wisdom that God is in all people, both good ones and bad ones, but that people are not in God unless they live in harmony with God's design. Jesus did say that he wanted us to be in him, and he in us. (John 15:4).

The more we let ourselves be brought into harmony with the divine pattern, the more God is fully present in every part of us, and the more God is in us, and we in God. "

Think of some things in nature. Where can you see something about God in each of them? For example, water flows in the same way that God's love flows into us.

●　●　○　○　○　●　●

Following God means being led by God

The common way of saying that "I follow God" is only real when we are also seeing and turning against our own natural wrongs and desires. There is no other way than this to be really following God.

> Following God means being led by God and not by ourselves.

It's impossible to be led by God unless we are not being led by ourselves. We are led by ourselves when we do not avoid doing wrong because it is against the Bible and therefore against God, meaning it is wrong and comes from hell. If we do not avoid and reject wrongdoing, we are being led by ourselves.

Why? Because these wrongs are within us from birth. They shape our life, because it is a life centred on ourselves. Before we reject these wrongs, everything we do comes from them, which means it comes from our self.

It is very different when we push those wrongs away, which happens when we avoid them because they are hellish. Then God enters into us with truth and goodness from heaven, and leads us.

... All this shows what it means to 'follow God wherever God goes' ...

... It is very different when we push those wrongs away ... then God enters into us with truth and goodness from heaven, and leads us ... page 93

The main reason for this is that each of us is our own love. Our spirit, which continues to live after death, is nothing but the temperament that goes with what we love. Every wrong comes from the love of it, meaning that it *is* that love. This means that our love or temperament can't be reshaped except by spiritually avoiding and rejecting wrongs, which is avoiding and rejecting them because they are hellish. All this shows what it means to 'follow God wherever God goes.'

All religion can be seen on one level as a way of life. Try to come up with several examples of how believing in God can make a difference in everyday life.

Doing good for the sake of God and for its own sake

Everyone would surely agree that doing good is right, but the reasons for doing good may well vary. The true reason we can do good is because it is from God, who is good itself.

> People who are led by the Devil provide useful services from selfish and materialistic motives. But people who are led by God are motivated by God and heaven to provide useful services. Everyone who avoids doing wrong because it is wrong provides useful services from God. But everyone who does not avoid doing wrong because it is wrong provides useful services from the Devil. That's because evil is the Devil, and useful service, or good, is God. This is the only way to tell the difference. Outwardly, they both appear to be the same. But inwardly they are completely different. One is like gold that has slag inside it. The other is like gold that has pure gold inside it. One is like artificial fruit that superficially looks like fruit from a tree when really it is just coloured wax that has powder or tar inside it. The other is like fine fruit that tastes and smells delicious, and has seeds inside.

What do you get from the idea that all good comes from God and is God?

• • ○ ○ ○ • •

... *One is like artificial fruit that superficially looks like fruit from a tree when really it has powder or tar inside it. The other tastes and smells delicious, and has seeds inside ...* page 96

It's important to see that God fights for us

A very important spiritual principle for us is that we recognise it is God who fights for us in our spiritual battles, even though we seem to be fighting the battle ourselves. But being like this, there can then be a conflict for us to meet, and as a result, we can be reformed.

> When we fight against our wrongs, we do have to fight as if we were on our own. Otherwise we will not fight at all. We'll just stand there like a robot without seeing or doing anything. We'll keep right on thinking based on our wrong desires and in favour of them rather than against them.
>
> However, we should understand clearly that it is only God who is fighting within us against our wrongs. It only appears to us as if we are fighting from our own strength. And God does want us to think this, because if we don't there will be no battle and no improvement in our character.

How can it be possible that we fight wrongs yet we know that it is God who fights the wrongs?

• • ○ ○ ○ • •

Asking for God's help brings God's help

When we turn from our wrongs because they go against the good and truth of God, we can then ask God to help us to resist them, and we will be helped. But if we don't turn from them they will keep getting stronger.

> We must focus on God, recognizing that every good thing that comes from love and all our understanding of truth that goes with wisdom comes from God, and none of it from ourselves. This is how we can make our character right, turning away from ourselves and toward God. This is how we can return to the form in which we were created—which was as receivers of what is good and true from God, and not at all from ourselves.

How helpful do you think it is to know that doing wrong goes against God rather than just being a fault that wounds our life?

... murder means all types of hostility, hatred, and desire for revenge. Murder hides within these like embers on a log buried under the ashes ... page 101

Different levels of what murder means

There are different levels of murder, from actual killing to harming beliefs to hating God. They are all connected together because they all come from the same source that is hell. In itself, hell is self-love and anger against all others.

" We love our neighbour exactly as much as we turn away from all types of murder because it is wrong.

All types of murder means all types of hostility, hatred, and desire for revenge, which breathe out a death wish. Murder hides within these like embers on a log buried under the ashes. That's exactly what hellfire is. That's where we get idioms like 'blazing with anger' and 'burning with revenge.' These things relate to murder in an earthly sense. But spiritually, murder means the many and varied ways we kill and destroy people's souls. And in the highest sense, murder means hating God. These three kinds of murder join forces in a common bond. Anyone who wants to kill another person's body in the world also wants to kill that person's soul after death—and also wants to kill God, burning with rage against God and wanting to snuff out God's name. "

How would you put the opposite of feeling murderous into words so as to show the contrast?

· · o O o · ·

Different levels of what adultery means

Actual adultery is breaking the sacredness of marriage with a sexual relationship outside it. The wrongfulness of that is reflected in all other kinds of adulteration of what is good, true and Divine.

> We love sexual purity exactly as much as we turn away from all kinds of unfaithfulness because it is wrong.
>
> In the Ten Commandments, the commandment against adultery in its earthly sense means not only sexual infidelity, but also obscene behavior, lewd talk, and filthy thoughts. In a spiritual sense, however, adultery means corrupting what is good in the Bible, and twisting its truth. And in its highest sense, adultery means denying God's divinity and corrupting the Bible. These are all the different kinds of unfaithfulness.
>
> Even materialistic people can know based on the light of reason that unfaithfulness also means obscene behavior, lewd talk, and filthy thoughts. But such people do not know that unfaithfulness also means corrupting what is good in the Bible and twisting its truth, still less that it means denying God's divinity and corrupting the Bible. Since they don't know these things, they don't realize that adultery is such a great evil that it could be called diabolical. Anyone who is engaged in earthly unfaithfulness is also engaged in spiritual unfaithfulness, and vice versa. And yet, people who do not consider unfaithfulness to be wrong in their minds and lives are engaged in all kinds of unfaithfulness at once.

*... In a spiritual sense, adultery
means corrupting what is good in
the Bible, and twisting its truth.
And in its highest sense, adultery
means denying God's divinity ...*

Think of a spiritual truth or teaching. How could it be turned,
bent or twisted to mean or justify the opposite of it?

• • o O o • •

Different levels of what stealing means

Stealing means taking away something belonging to someone else. Stealing spiritually means taking someone's belief or love from them, and stealing from God means claiming for ourselves what belongs to God.

> **We love honesty exactly as much as we turn away from all kinds of theft because it is wrong.**
>
> **In an earthly sense, theft means not only thieving and robbing, but also defrauding people and taking their belongings away from them through various scams. In a spiritual sense, though, it means taking away other people's belief in what is true and their good life of kindness to others. In the highest sense theft means transferring what is God's to ourselves and giving ourselves credit for it, claiming that we are righteous and worthy in our own right.**
>
> **These are all the different kinds of theft. They work together just as all the different kinds of unfaithfulness and all the different kinds of murder do. They join forces in a common bond because each one lurks within the others.**

Any stealing involves knowing that something belongs to another person. With that idea, think about the practical wrong done to another person in harming their belief or their love.

· · ○ ○ ○ · ·

Using our mind to make real choices

We have the ability to reason, to look at things this way and that, and to form conclusions. This is God's gift to us; by means of it we can see what things are wrong and we can choose to turn against them. Doing this allows reason to lead us.

> Using our capability known as rationality, we can figure out what good things are useful to the community in the spiritual world, and what bad things are harmful there, if we think of bad things as offences, and of good things as acts of kindness. We can do this, if we want to, using our rational abilities because we do have rationality and freedom. Our rationality and freedom are uncovered, make their appearance, guide us, and give us the ability to understand things and act just as much as we avoid those bad things because they are wrong. And as much as we do this, we look at the good things of kindness the way a neighbour looks at a neighbour, from mutual love.

Sound reason tells us that God wants everything we do in freedom based on our own rational thought to appear

*... Our rationality and freedom
are uncovered, guiding us and giving
us the ability to understand things and
act to avoid those bad things because
they are wrong ...*

as if it belonged to us because this makes it possible for us to accept God into ourselves and build a relationship with God. We can therefore be motivated to do this based on rational thought, knowing that it leads to our eternal happiness. Then, when we turn to God for the strength we need, we can accomplish it. ”

Think about some situation in life that you can see from different angles, and then think about a situation in life where you are adamant about its rightness or wrongness.

Spiritual self-discipline, or none

In the same way that society has to manage people who commit crimes so that society can function, we need to be disciplined about ourselves, not only in our outward behaviour but in our private thoughts and emotions as well.

> **Consider the widespread corruption that has taken hold in human society. Unless criminals were disciplined and punished by the law, no city or nation could survive.**
>
> **Each of us is like a human community in miniature. If we don't deal with ourselves spiritually in the same way criminals are dealt with physically in the wider community, after death we will be disciplined and punished. This will continue until we no longer do wrong out of fear of being punished—although we can never be induced to do good from any love of it.**

Can you suggest several ways in which we can rightly go about disciplining ourselves?

• • ○ ○ ○ • •

... Each of us is like a human community in miniature ...

... like cutting down a bad tree and leaving its roots in the ground. From those roots the same bad tree will grow all over again, spreading itself all around ... page 109

Examining our heart, not just our life

Real work on ourselves needs us to search our intentions and deal with them. To rein in only behaviour and speech is not going far enough, even though we seem different than before.

> **The real work of being sorry for our wrongdoing involves looking closely not only at our actions, but also at our motives and intentions. It is our motivation and our understanding that lead to our actions. We speak from what we understand, and we act from our motives. In other words, our words are our thoughts speaking, and our actions are our motives acting. Since these are the source of our words and actions, there is no doubt that when our body does something wrong, it is our motivation and understanding that are doing something wrong.**
>
> **Yes, it is possible for us to stop doing wrong physically while still thinking and wanting what is wrong. But this is like cutting down a bad tree and leaving its roots in the ground. From those roots the same bad tree will grow all over again, spreading itself all around.**
>
> **It is different when we also pull out the roots. We do this when we look closely at our intentions as well, and get rid of our wrongs by doing the work of being sorry for them.**

Think about searching our intentions. How can we best begin doing that so that we see them?

• • O O O • •

About being like a barren landscape or a fertile landscape

This quote gives the example of a barren landscape which, when it has been cleared of terrifying creatures residing there, can then be made fertile.

> **Before we have done the work of being sorry for our wrongdoing, we are like a barren landscape where there are terrifying creatures. Hiding in the thickets are the wild beasts of the desert mentioned in the Bible—and all the while, demons are dancing.**
>
> **However, if we put in the human energy and labour required to reclaim that barren landscape, it can once again become fertile land where forests and crops grow.**

Can you relate this illustration to how your personal life and outlook can be radically changed from one way of thinking to a very different one? Is it a once-for-all change or more an ongoing thing?

• • ○ ○ ○ • •

Doing good for gain is actually a craving

We can certainly do good actions just for our own glory and its delight, but this is a kind of hell, and it becomes a craving. Spirits who live in hell have no love for doing good, but they must do good, so as to be fed and provided for.

> Yes, we could do good deeds of useful service out of a love for praise, reputation, profit, and their pleasures. But then we are not embodiments of kindness. Instead, we are embodiments of craving. Then we are not manifestations of heaven, but manifestations of hell. Even in hell, everyone has to do good deeds. But there they don't do it out of friendliness. They are forced to.

When you feel you just can't start something but you have to, what kind of thoughts and feelings help you?

· · o O o · ·

... But then we are not embodiments of kindness. Instead, we are embodiments of craving ...

Not asking what is good but what is wrong

When we turn against our own wrongs we create space to see what is good. So it is far better to start there than to start by asking what good we can do.

> When we avoid doing wrong because it is wrong, we learn every day what is good and right for us to do. An enjoyment in doing good grows in us, as does an enjoyment in knowing the truth for the sake of what is good. The more we know of the truth, the more abundantly and wisely we can do things, so that our actions become truly good.
>
> Stop asking yourself, then, 'What good deeds can I do, and what good thing must I do to receive eternal life?' Just avoid doing wrong because it is wrong and focus on God, and God will teach you and guide you.

Do you think people think more about doing good things rather than stopping doing wrong things? Why do you think it's like this?

The ladder of the motivations for good

There is a progression in our feelings towards good and evil. The first is linked with fear, the next with a horror about wrongdoing, and the last is a love for what is good and true, which is of God.

> It is good to be aware that each one of us, when we start living a spiritual life because we want to be saved, is afraid of doing wrong because we don't want to get punished in hell. But as time goes on, we are afraid of the wrongdoing itself because it truly is hellish. And eventually, we avoid doing wrong because of the truth and goodness that we love—meaning we avoid it for the sake of God. As much as we love what is true and good, we love God, and we also reject their opposite, which is evil.
>
> This shows that when we believe in God, we avoid doing wrong because it is wrong. Conversely, when we avoid doing wrong because it is wrong, we believe in God. In short, avoiding wrongdoing because it is wrong is a sign of faith.

How do you think this progression or ladder helps us in our spiritual life and practice?

Now we're at the end of the book let's check things. The aim of the book is to bring together spiritual ideas and our life that goes on inside us. This matters a lot because it's relevant. It helps each of us personally, and gets us involved with the spiritual things being talked about. It's good too if it has shown us things we never saw or knew about before.

One thing comes up all the time in the book: how we need to see our wrongs and understand how we can manage them. Of course, it is true that each one of us has our wrongs. These wrongs help us see that we are human and we get things wrong at times or we treat other people unfairly. It's our wrongs that are bad. It's not about blaming ourselves but seeing them, then choosing to want them out of our life and doing our best, with God's help.

Doing that will be challenging, but it's good to be challenged and stretched. It wakes us up, it brings opportunities, and it makes us more attentive to everything. This is something we take part in every day, and the outcome is to know ourselves more and to like who we are, and to like other people being who they are. It's about all of us being okay being human.

• • o O o • •

EXPLORE *further*

Where the quotes come from

Each quote in this book is taken from one of the books written by Emanuel Swedenborg. Below is a list giving the source for every quote. Firstly the page number and quote heading in this book, then the title of the book it was taken from, followed by the section number in that book (see the disclaimer on page 2.)

For a full list of books by Emanuel Swedenborg and how to access these books, see pages 124 and 125.

Page 8   **We must look into ourselves**, quote taken from *New Jerusalem* sections 159 to 161

Page 9   **We must look closely**, quote taken from *New Jerusalem* section 162

Page 10   **We must look honestly**, quote taken from *New Jerusalem* section 164

Page 11   **We must look regularly**, quote taken from *New Jerusalem* section 163

Page 13   **We need to live out our wish to change**, quote taken from *New Jerusalem* section 165

Page 14   **Tangible signs of us changing**, quote taken from *New Jerusalem* section 167

Page 15   **Clear signs nothing has changed**, quote taken from *New Jerusalem* section 167

Page 16   **What goes from us only gets shelved**, quote taken from *New Jerusalem* section 166

Page 17   **Changing freely as against being compelled**, quote taken from *New Jerusalem* section 168

Page 18   **We need to keep this whole process going**, quote taken from *New Jerusalem* section 169

Page 19   **The real purpose of religion**, quote taken from *Life* section 27

Page 21   **Everything religious is about our life**, quote taken from *Life* section 8

Page 22   **Our two core spiritual needs**, quote taken from *Charity* section 58

• • ○ ○ ○ • •

Emanuel Swedenborg (1688–1772), the source of the quotes in this book, was a spiritual writer in the eighteenth century. In Europe, this was the age of reason, and many established religious beliefs were being re-examined. Swedenborg's development was one of a strong childhood sense of God and angels, a classical education, a major interest and involvement in the sciences of the day, a practical ability to invent, a seat in Sweden's parliament, and a position on its national Board of Mines. When he was with others, he was regarded as sociable and kind, with a clear mind and a friendly disposition.

The last thirty years of Swedenborg's life, however, were entirely given over to the things of spiritual life: to things about God, eternal life, the meaning of the Bible, the created world, and most of all, our inner spiritual life and growth. Swedenborg saw us as beings capable of receiving the life and light of God, each in our own way. For Swedenborg, real religion is embedded in life, in active living based on understanding that we receive life from God. We are to

live responsibly, with goodness and usefulness being
our purpose.

Swedenborg's earlier scientific interest and research was
a valuable lead-in for his spiritual writing. His wide experience
in researching geology, cosmology, astronomy and especially
anatomy trained him in being meticulous, and at times
gave him an ability to propose causes and results which
have been found to be correct. When he was led to focus
on spiritual things, he was able to bring the same wide
detailed and connected approach to his explanations.
For Swedenborg, God is universally present in absolutely
everything, even though the physical world appears to exist
from itself.

Swedenborg wrote extensively during these thirty years, and
published his writings at his own expense. He sent copies to
people he felt would find his concepts interesting and well-
founded. Swedenborg said he received all his spiritual
teachings from God, who led his mind to see what is true.
He writes that it was God who opened his mind for the
purpose of explaining the spiritual meaning of scripture, but
which then broadened into other matters over time. He was
shown the spiritual world, the world of the afterlife, where he
witnessed many things. He did not advocate making contact
with this spiritual world that he witnessed, because this is not
meant for us in this life, and could harm the divine intention
for our lives.

Since Swedenborg's time, many people have found his
spiritual writings to be helpful and inspiring. Many famous

people have appreciated his approach and coverage of spiritual realities, including Helen Keller, Johnny Appleseed, William Blake, Arthur Conan Doyle, Elizabeth Barrett Browning, Honoré de Balzac, Ralph Waldo Emerson, Jorge Luis Borges, Dr Eben Alexander, Kenneth Ring, Carl Jung, Norman Vincent Peale, Colin Wilson, C.S. Lewis, and many others.

For Swedenborg, we are already in the spiritual world in our mind and heart, our thoughts and emotions, and we come into it completely when our physical life ends.

• • ○ O ○ • •

Books by Emanuel Swedenborg

Below is a list of the spiritual books written and published by Emanuel Swedenborg. The titles are the ones used in the New Century Edition, which is the most recent edition of Swedenborg's works, followed by the traditional title if it is different from the New Century Edition title. These books are available from the Swedenborg Foundation at swedenborg.com/bookstore and also as searchable online texts at newchristianbiblestudy.org/swedenborg

Books published by Emanuel Swedenborg

Divine Love and Wisdom

Divine Providence

Faith, traditional title: *The Doctrine of Faith*

Heaven and Hell

Last Judgment, traditional title: *The Last Judgment*

Life, traditional title: *The Doctrine of Life*

The Lord, traditional title: *The Doctrine of the Lord*

Marriage Love, traditional title: *Conjugial Love*

New Jerusalem, traditional title: *The New Jerusalem and its Heavenly Doctrine*

Other Planets, traditional title: *Earths in the Universe*

Revelation Unveiled, traditional title: *Apocalypse Revealed*

Sacred Scripture, traditional title: *The Doctrine of the Sacred Scripture*

Secrets of Heaven, traditional title: *Arcana Caelestia*

Soul-Body Interaction, traditional title: *Interaction of the Soul and the Body*

Supplements on the Last Judgment and the Spiritual World, traditional title: *Continuation of the Last Judgment*

Survey, traditional title: *Brief Exposition*

True Christianity, traditional title: *True Christian Religion*

White Horse, traditional title *The White Horse*

Books by Emanuel Swedenborg published after his death

Here is a partial list of books that Swedenborg wrote but did not publish. These are available only in earlier editions.

Apocalypse Explained
Canons of the New Church
Charity
Coronis
De Verbo
Divine Love and Divine Wisdom
Last Judgment (Posthumous)
Spiritual Experiences (traditional title: *Spiritual Diary)*

Basil Lazer began offering selected quotes from Emanuel Swedenborg's spiritual writings when he believed with a real earnestness that these quotes would be helpful to people and add meaning to their lives. His hope was that many people would be as captivated as he had been in first coming across them.

To fulfil that goal, Basil began to select quotes and arrange them in booklet form, letting the quotes speak for themselves, but at times offering his own commentary and excitement. He funded the production of these booklets himself, and covered the cost of sending them to people in Australia and overseas, sometimes in considerable numbers, particularly to Africa, where they were taken up with great joy.

When Basil left this life, his will included an amount of money so that his booklets could continue to be produced. A directive in the will led to setting up The Basil Lazer Trust to carry out this work. These current editions show Basil's vision brought into a contemporary context with modern clear language.

Basil was born into an ultra-orthodox Jewish family in East Melbourne, Victoria, Australia in 1909. His mother had been widowed during her pregnancy with him and the family lived in poverty. Basil was the youngest of five children. His childhood and school life were miserable, unhappy years. He was teased at school and was constantly fearful. Because he was a Jew he was taught to hate Jesus and that the New Testament was lies which he was forbidden to read under threat of damnation. In adulthood he was led to Christianity and embraced it. Within the teachings of Christianity, Basil discovered that God is loving and not angry.

One day while on holiday, Basil was introduced to someone who like him was seeking answers. This person told him that he had received a book describing the afterlife in both heaven and hell. Basil was astounded that this could be possible, and wrote for a copy of the book, which was Emanuel Swedenborg's *Heaven and Hell*. As he read it, he says that it gripped him with its teaching that what a person loves and

... Living a life of kindness and faith means doing the work of being sorry for our wrongs every day, paying attention to the faults in our character, admitting them, not acting on them, and asking God for help ...

desires most of all manifests after death and leads him or her to seek a life and community in accord with that.

Basil then read all of Swedenborg's writings, which gave him a cohesive understanding of God, eternal life, regeneration, usefulness, good and evil, and the deeper meaning of the Bible. This gave birth to his determination to bring these great spiritual treasures to people, some of whom, he felt, would be overjoyed at finding such answers to their own existence. He never let up from this commission, which he felt God had placed with him. He found personal joy in serving a purpose in life for God's greater purposes, and he did it well, and provided for its continuing future.

Those who knew Basil described him as an amiable, kindly gentleman who, although he remained single, was 'Uncle Basil' to the children of the families who became his friends. He left this life in 1991 at the age of eighty two, in Canberra, the capital of Australia, his home and place of employment in his younger years.

● ● ○ ⃝ ○ ● ●

About Lee Woofenden

Lee Woofenden has translated each of the quotes in this book from the Latin writings of Emanuel Swedenborg into contemporary English. He aims to make Swedenborg's ideas readable and relatable for ordinary people by putting them into the language in which we think and talk today.

Lee has a long history of translating and editing Swedenborg's works, including many years working for the Swedenborg Foundation in America. Rendering spiritual ideas that are often abstract and subtle into immediately understandable English is no mean feat. We are delighted with his wonderful translations for this book. Lee's writing based on the Bible and Swedenborg can be found on his blog, *Spiritual Insights for Everyday Life* at leewoof.org

• • o O o • •

... On our own, we are always going downhill. But God is always lifting us up and leading us towards what is good ...

www.oursharedspirituality.org